Ms. Sally's

Healthy Habit

CALENDAR JOURNAL

Ms. Sally's

Healthy Habit

CALENDAR JOURNAL

For Kids

TEACHER'S GUIDE

SALLY BRADLEY

A Ms. Sally Book-www.Leemitt.com

Printed in the United States of America

Publishing services by Selah Publishing Group, LLC, Tennessee. The views expressed or implied in this work do not necessarily reflect those of Selah Publishing Group.

ISBN: 978-1-58930-252-5
Library of Congress Control Number: 2010903105

To Teachers:

The major pursuit of "Ms. Sally's Healthy Habit Calendar Journals for kids is to help grow their minds with positive inputs to make better choices and goals for themselves.

This journal is also designed for interactive dialogue and open discussions.

"To believe in a child is to believe in the future.
Through their aspirations they will save the world.
With their combined knowledge the turbulent seas of hate and injustice will be calmed. They will champion the causes of life's underdogs, forging a society without class discrimination. They will supply humanity with the music and beauty, as it has never known. They will endure. Towards these ends I pledge my life's work.

I will supply the children with tools and knowledge to overcome the obstacles. I will pass on the wisdom of my years and temper it with patience. I shall impact in each child the desire to fulfill his or her dream.

I shall teach."

– Henry James

For Teachers

INTRODUCTION

According to "America's Children: Key National Indicators of Well-Being," adolescent participation in high- risk or illegal behaviors can have severe, long-term consequences for our youth and our society.

These behaviors include cigarette smoking, drinking alcohol, using illicit drugs, engaging in sexual activity and participating in violent crimes.

According to the "National Health and Nutrition Examination Survey," 19% of 6-11 year olds are overweight.

Ms. Sally's Healthy Habit Calendar Journal has been designed to reduce the dramatic increase in negative input that produces horrible effects in a youth's life both emotionally and physically.

This journal will:

- Target 3rd thru 7th graders
- Promote positive self-image and healthy choices
- Build confidence, self-esteem and proper behavior patterns
- Help children learn to set goals and plan effectively
- Promote healthier eating habits
- Provide a good foundation for life skills
- Motivate and problem solve through role playing
- Enhance reading and writing skills

Ms. Sally's Healthy Habit Calendar Journal is separated into four-week sessions, which include:

POSITIVE WORD SEED: The students will be given the "POSITIVE WORD SEED" for the entire month. Students become what they program in their minds. With positive repetition students will have the ability to make better choices in life.

- **1st week**: ACTION STEPS section. In this section the teacher and the students will come up with some practical steps to incorporate the "POSITIVE WORD SEED" into their everyday lives at school, home, etc. This will help promote students to become more active in their writing, problem solving and planning skills.

- **2nd week**: POSITIVE REINFORCEMENT section. In this section the students will be able to reinforce the word of the month through encouraging one another by discussing the positive/negative consequences they may have for applying or not applying the "POSITIVE WORD SEED" of the month into their daily lives. This will build confidence, self-esteem, communication and healthy attitudes.

- **3rd week**: ROLE-PLAYING section. This is a fun way to motivate children to learn and problem solve. Teachers and students will come up with short skits for the "POSITIVE WORD SEED."

- **4th week**: GROWING section. In the last week for the "POSITIVE WORD SEED" of the month, the students will start growing from the inside, out, by remembering and using the "POSITIVE WORD SEED" in their everyday lives. This will help build a stronger foundation for a positive self-image, and proper behavior patterns.

Note: The students will have their own personal "Ms. Sally's Healthy Habit Calendar Journal" to write in.

Teacher Directed Mini Lessons

Each month you will have a POSITIVE WORD SEED that the students will be focusing on and developing through repetition, writing, interactiveness and open discussion.

For example: dealing with their Attitudes towards others, Patience, Communication, etc.

- In the first week, have the students state their plans in the "ACTION STEPS" section, listing specific daily actions that will help them become better people and students, demonstrating and using the "POSITIVE WORD SEED" of the month.

- In the second week, encourage the students in the "POSITIVE REINFORCEMENT" section of the journal by having them check one another's progress as well as their own. Have the entire class of students' names on pieces of paper, placed in a hat, have each student pull one name out of the hat, and have them encourage each other in pairs. Or, you can have an open discussion with the entire class. This is a great opportunity to talk on topics like: problem solving, respect, self-esteem, etc.

- In the third week, the "ROLE-PLAYING" section is a fun and simple way to motivate students. Have the students come up with short skits for the "POSITIVE WORD SEED" of the month. Have them act out the related word.

Example: The "POSITIVE WORD SEED" is Thankful. Have the students come up with a short skit using the word Thankful, such as when receiving, or having the opportunity to give someone a gift.

- In the fourth week, the "GROWING" section will be the last week of focus on the "POSITIVE WORD SEED" of the month. Have each student write in the "GROWING" section how the "POSITIVE WORD SEED" has made him or her more confident and how he or she will continue to use the "POSITIVE WORD SEED."

Positive Seed Word

January: <u>Attitude</u>

This month introduces children to the "Positive Word Seed" path with focus on developing positive attitudes.

February: <u>Behavior</u>

This month encourages conscientious action and the building of good character.

March: <u>Nutrition</u>

This month will focus on making healthy eating choices and exercise.

- March is National Nutrition Month.

April: <u>Communication</u>

In April the children will discover the importance of interacting and communicating respectfully and effectively to learning and living.

May: <u>Table Manners</u>

This month will focus on manners at the table.

June: <u>Listening</u>

This is the month to teach the children that being a good listener is an essential among life skills.

July: Read

While school is out, this is the month to read a positive book. Have the children write about what they have read and how the book encouraged and helped them.

August: Sharing

This is the month to demonstrate sharing to others.

September: Respect

This is usually when children return to school and they may have formed some bad habits during their vacation time. This is a great time to establish respect for others and themselves.

October: Think

This is the month to have them think before they react to situations.

November: Thankful

This is the month to focus on being thankful for each other.

December: Growth

This is the month will be the focus of growth in there lives.

Kids' Quote

"Motivation is what gets you started.
Habit is what keeps you going."

— Anonymous

JANUARY

The Positive Word Seed: Attitude

TEACHERS:
Other words: happy, patient, kind, and thoughtful.

at·ti·tude
Pronunciation: \ˈa-tə-ˌtüd, -ˌtyüd\
Function: *noun*
Etymology: French, from Italian *attitudine,* literally, aptitude, from Late Latin *aptitudin-, aptitudo* fitness
Date: 1668

1 : the arrangement of the parts of a body or figure : posture
2 : a position assumed for a specific purpose <a threatening attitude>
3 : a ballet position similar to the arabesque in which the raised leg is bent at the knee
4 a : a mental position with regard to a fact or state <a helpful attitude>
b : a feeling or emotion toward a fact or state
5 : the position of an aircraft or spacecraft determined by the relationship between its axes and a reference datum (as the horizon or a particular star)
6 : an organismic state of readiness to respond in a characteristic way to a stimulus (as an object, concept, or situation)
7 a : a negative or hostile state of mind
b : a cool, cocky, defiant, or arrogant manner

"The only difference between a Good Day
And a Bad Day is your ATTITUDE!"

– Dennis S. Brown

Action Steps

☐ Sunday ______________________

☐ Monday ______________________

☐ Tuesday ______________________

☐ Wednesday ______________________

☐ Thursday ______________________

☐ Friday ______________________

☐ Saturday ______________________

Positive Reinforcement

☐ Sunday ______________________________

____

____

☐ Monday ______________________________

____

____

☐ Tuesday ______________________________

____

____

☐ Wednesday ______________________________

____

____

☐ Thursday ______________________________

____

____

☐ Friday ______________________________

____

____

☐ Saturday ______________________________

____

____

Role Playing

☐ Sunday ______________________________

____

____

☐ Monday ______________________________

____

____

☐ Tuesday ______________________________

____

____

☐ Wednesday ______________________________

____

____

☐ Thursday ______________________________

____

____

☐ Friday ______________________________

____

____

☐ Saturday ______________________________

____

____

January

Attitude

Week 4

Growing

☐ Sunday

☐ Monday

☐ Tuesday

☐ Wednesday

☐ Thursday

☐ Friday

☐ Saturday

January

Notes

January Notes cont.

FEBRUARY

The Positive Word Seed: Behavior

TEACHERS:
Other words: kindness, character and politeness.

be·hav·ior
Pronunciation: \bi-'hā-vyər, bē-\
Function: *noun*
Etymology: alteration of Middle English *behavour*, from *behaven*
Date: 15th century

1 a : the manner of conducting oneself
  b : anything that an organism does involving action and response to stimulation
  c : the response of an individual, group, or species to its environment
2 : the way in which someone behaves; ***also*** : an instance of such behavior
3 : the way in which something functions or operates
— be·hav·ior·al \-vyə-rəl\ *adjective*
— be·hav·ior·al·ly \-rə-lē\ *adverb*

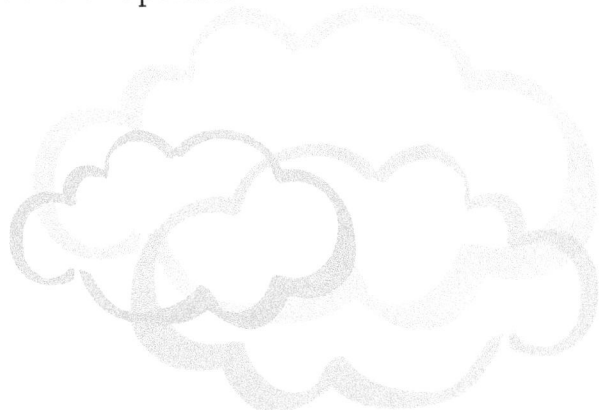

Teacher's Quote

"Do the right things at the right time for the right reasons."

– Leonard Chitunhu

Kids' Quote

"There's never a wrong time to do what's right."

- Unknown

Action Steps

☐ Sunday ______

☐ Monday ______

☐ Tuesday ______

☐ Wednesday ______

☐ Thursday ______

☐ Friday ______

☐ Saturday ______

Positive Reinforcement

☐ Sunday ______________________________

____

____

☐ Monday ______________________________

____

____

☐ Tuesday ______________________________

____

____

☐ Wednesday ______________________________

____

____

☐ Thursday ______________________________

____

____

☐ Friday ______________________________

____

____

☐ Saturday ______________________________

____

____

Role Playing

☐ Sunday ______________________________

____

____

☐ Monday ______________________________

____

____

☐ Tuesday ______________________________

____

____

☐ Wednesday ______________________________

____

____

☐ Thursday ______________________________

____

____

☐ Friday ______________________________

____

____

☐ Saturday ______________________________

____

____

February Behavior week 4

Growing

☐ Sunday ____________________

☐ Monday ____________________

☐ Tuesday ____________________

☐ Wednesday ____________________

☐ Thursday ____________________

☐ Friday ____________________

☐ Saturday ____________________

February

Notes

February Notes cont.

MARCH

The Positive Word Seed: Nutrition

TEACHERS:
Other words: health, fitness, metabolism and growth.

nu·tri·tion
Pronunciation: \nu̇-ˈtri-shən, nyu̇-\
Function: *noun*
Etymology: Middle English *nutricioun*, from Late Latin *nutrition-*, *nutritio*, from Latin *nutrire*
Date: 15th century

1 : the act or process of nourishing or being nourished; *specifically* : the sum of the processes by which an animal or plant takes in and utilizes food substances

2 : nourishment 1

— nu·tri·tion·al \-ˈtrish-nəl, -ˈtri-shə-nəl\ *adjective*

— nu·tri·tion·al·ly *adverb*

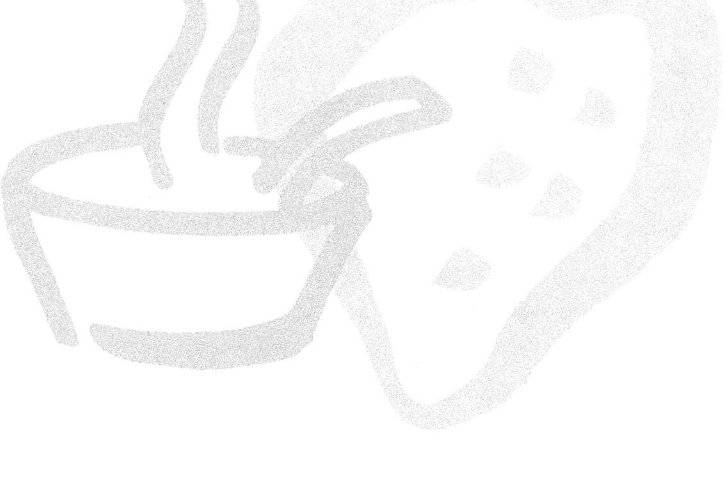

Kids' Quote

"Don't be the one you see
but the one you want to be."

-Unknown

Action Steps

☐ Sunday ______________________________

____

____

☐ Monday ______________________________

____

____

☐ Tuesday ______________________________

____

____

☐ Wednesday ______________________________

____

____

☐ Thursday ______________________________

____

____

☐ Friday ______________________________

____

____

☐ Saturday ______________________________

____

____

Positive Reinforcement

☐ Sunday

☐ Monday

☐ Tuesday

☐ Wednesday

☐ Thursday

☐ Friday

☐ Saturday

Role Playing

☐ Sunday

☐ Monday

☐ Tuesday

☐ Wednesday

☐ Thursday

☐ Friday

☐ Saturday

March

Nutrition week 4

Growing

☐ Sunday

☐ Monday

☐ Tuesday

☐ Wednesday

☐ Thursday

☐ Friday

☐ Saturday

March

Notes

March Notes cont.

APRIL

The Positive Word Seed:

communication

TEACHERS:
Other words: talking, listening, words, compliment, "Excuse me", expression, handshake and smile.

com·mu·ni·ca·tion
Pronunciation: \kə-ˌmyü-nə-ˈkā-shən\
Function: *noun*
Date: 14th century

1 : an act or instance of transmitting
2 a : information communicated
   b : a verbal or written message
3 a : a process by which information is exchanged between individuals through a common system of symbols, signs, or behavior <the function of pheromones in insect communication>; *also* : exchange of information
   b : personal rapport <a lack of communication between old and young persons>
4 *plural*
   a : a system (as of telephones) for communicating
   b : a system of routes for moving troops, supplies, and vehicles
   c : personnel engaged in communicating
5 *plural but sing or plural in constr*
   a : a technique for expressing ideas effectively (as in speech)
   b : the technology of the transmission of information (as by print or telecommunication)

— com·mu·ni·ca·tion·al \-shnəl, -shə-nəl\ *adjective*

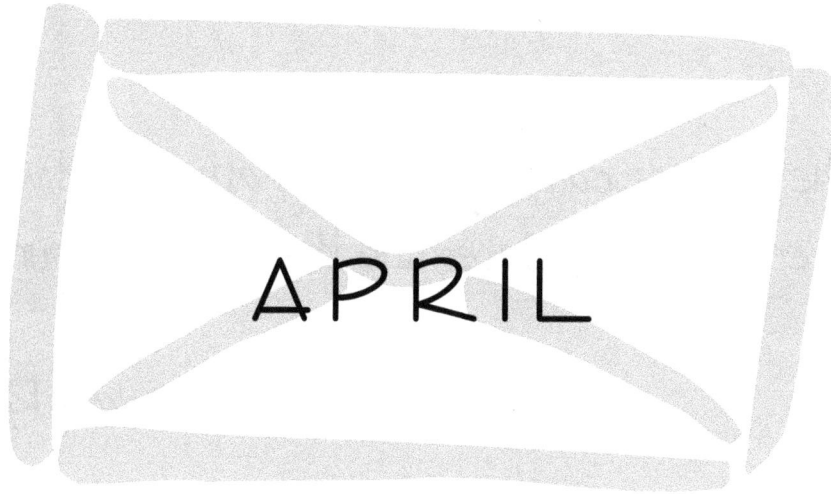

Teacher's Quote

"The way we communicate with others and with ourselves ultimately determine the quality of our lives."

– Anthony Robbins

Kids' Quote

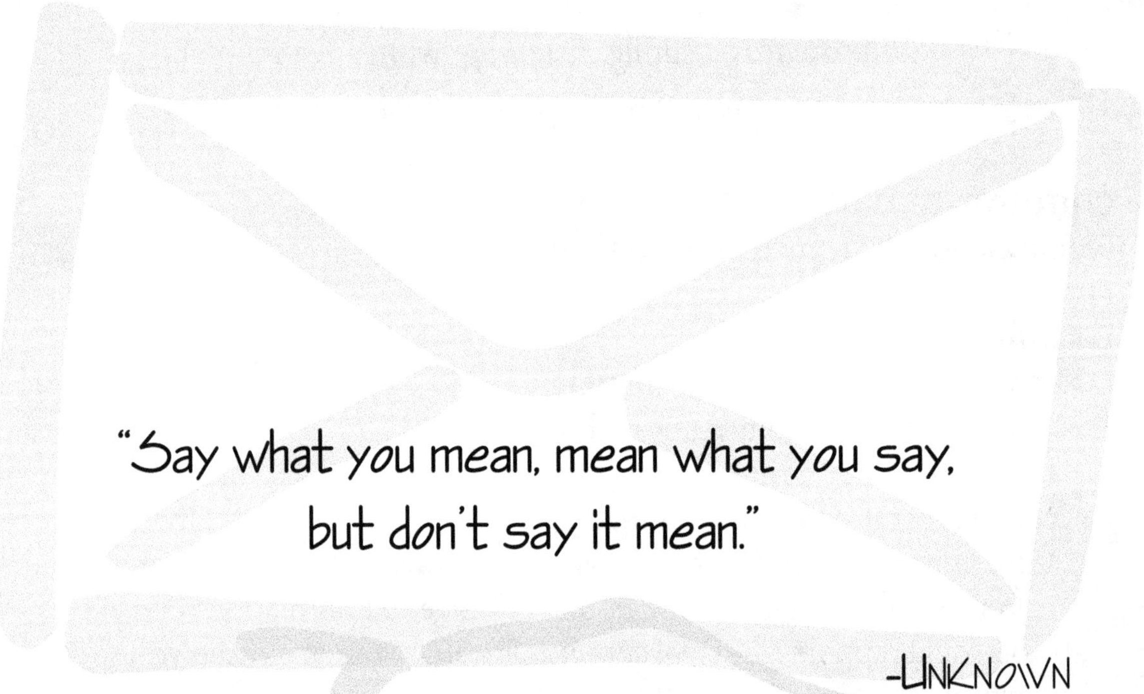

"Say what you mean, mean what you say, but don't say it mean."

-Unknown

Action Steps

☐ Sunday ______________________________

____

____

☐ Monday ______________________________

____

____

☐ Tuesday ______________________________

____

____

☐ Wednesday ______________________________

____

____

☐ Thursday ______________________________

____

____

☐ Friday ______________________________

____

____

☐ Saturday ______________________________

____

____

Positive Reinforcement

☐ Sunday

☐ Monday

☐ Tuesday

☐ Wednesday

☐ Thursday

☐ Friday

☐ Saturday

April

communication

week 3

Role Playing

☐ Sunday ______

______

______

☐ Monday ______

______

______

☐ Tuesday ______

______

______

☐ Wednesday ______

______

______

☐ Thursday ______

______

______

☐ Friday ______

______

______

☐ Saturday ______

______

______

April

Communication

week 4

Growing

☐ Sunday ______

☐ Monday ______

☐ Tuesday ______

☐ Wednesday ______

☐ Thursday ______

☐ Friday ______

☐ Saturday ______

April

Notes

April Notes cont.

MAY

The Positive Word Seed:

Table-Manners

TEACHERS:

Other words: courtesy, decorum, etiquette, politeness.

Table Manners: A pattern of behavior that is conventionally required of someone while eating.

man·ner

Pronunciation: \'ma-nər\

Function: *noun*

Etymology: Middle English *manere*, from Anglo-French, from Vulgar Latin **manuaria*, from Latin, feminine of *manuarius* of the hand, from *manus* hand — more at manual

Date: 12th century

1 a : kind, sort <what manner of man is he>
b : kinds, sorts <all manner of problems>

2 a (1) : a characteristic or customary mode of acting : custom (2) : a mode of procedure or way of acting : fashion (3) : method of artistic execution or mode of presentation : style
b plural : social conduct or rules of conduct as shown in the prevalent customs <Victorian manners>
c : characteristic or distinctive bearing, air, or deportment <his poised gracious manner> d *plural* (1) : habitual conduct or deportment : behavior <mind your manners> (2) : good manners e : a distinguished or stylish air

synonyms see bearing, method

— man·ner·less \-ləs\ *adjective*

Kids' Quote

"Manners are a mirror in which
One shows his portrait."

– Trenetta Robertson

Action Steps

☐ Sunday ______________________________

____

____

☐ Monday ______________________________

____

____

☐ Tuesday ______________________________

____

____

☐ Wednesday ______________________________

____

____

☐ Thursday ______________________________

____

____

☐ Friday ______________________________

____

____

☐ Saturday ______________________________

____

____

Positive Reinforcement

☐ Sunday ______________________________

☐ Monday ______________________________

☐ Tuesday ______________________________

☐ Wednesday ______________________________

☐ Thursday ______________________________

☐ Friday ______________________________

☐ Saturday ______________________________

Role Playing

☐ Sunday ________________________________

☐ Monday ________________________________

☐ Tuesday ________________________________

☐ Wednesday ________________________________

☐ Thursday ________________________________

☐ Friday ________________________________

☐ Saturday ________________________________

May

Table-Manners

week 4

Growing

Sunday

Monday

Tuesday

Wednesday

Thursday

Friday

Saturday

May

Notes

May Notes cont.

JUNE

The Positive Word Seed: Listening

TEACHERS:
Other words: attentive, concentrating and interested.

lis·ten

Pronunciation: \'li-sən\
Function: *verb*
Inflected Form(s): lis·tened; lis·ten·ing \'lis-niŋ, 'li-sən-iŋ\
Etymology: Middle English listnen, from Old English hlysnan; akin to Sanskrit **śroṣati** he hears, Old English **hlūd** loud
Date: before 12th century

transitive verb archaic : to give ear to :
hearintransitive verb

1 : to pay attention to sound <listen to music>
2 : to hear something with thoughtful attention : give consideration <listen to a plea>
3 : to be alert to catch an expected sound <listen for his step>

— lis·ten·er \'lis-nər, 'li-sən-ər\ *noun*

"God gave us two ears and one mouth,
So we can hear twice as much as we say."

– Unknown

June

Action Steps

Listening

Week 1

☐ Sunday ______

______

______

☐ Monday ______

______

______

☐ Tuesday ______

______

______

☐ Wednesday ______

______

______

☐ Thursday ______

______

______

☐ Friday ______

______

______

☐ Saturday ______

______

______

Positive Reinforcement

☐ Sunday

☐ Monday

☐ Tuesday

☐ Wednesday

☐ Thursday

☐ Friday

☐ Saturday

June

Listening

Week 3

Role Playing

☐ Sunday ____________________

☐ Monday ____________________

☐ Tuesday ____________________

☐ Wednesday ____________________

☐ Thursday ____________________

☐ Friday ____________________

☐ Saturday ____________________

June

Listening

Week 4

Growing

☐ Sunday ______________________________

____

____

☐ Monday ______________________________

____

____

☐ Tuesday ______________________________

____

____

☐ Wednesday ______________________________

____

____

☐ Thursday ______________________________

____

____

☐ Friday ______________________________

____

____

☐ Saturday ______________________________

____

____

June

Notes

June Notes cont.

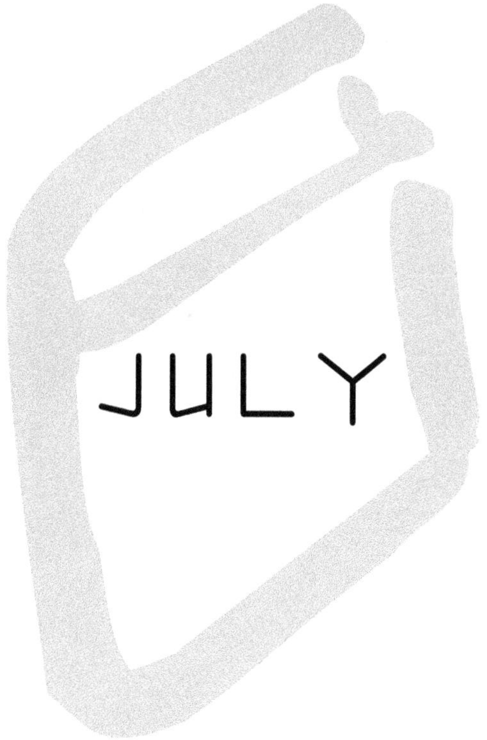

JULY

The Positive Word Seed: Read

TEACHERS:

Other words: comprehend, discover, learn and study.

read

Pronunciation: \'**rēd**\

Function: *verb*

Inflected Form(s): **read** \'**red**\; read·ing \'**rē-diŋ**\

Etymology: Middle English **reden** to advise, interpret, read, from Old English **rǣdan**; akin to Old High German **rātan** to advise, Sanskrit **rādhnoti** he achieves, prepares

Date: before 12th century

transitive verb

1 a (1) : to receive or take in the sense of (as letters or symbols) especially by sight or touch (2) : to study the movements of (as lips) with mental formulation of the communication expressed (3) : to utter aloud the printed or written words of <read them a story>

b : to learn from what one has seen or found in writing or printing

c : to deliver aloud by or as if by reading; *specifically* : to utter interpretively

d (1) : to become acquainted with or look over the contents of (as a book) (2) : to make a study of <read law> (3) : to read the works of

e : to check (as copy or proof) for errors f (1) : to receive and understand (a voice message) by radio (2) : To understand.

Kids' Quote

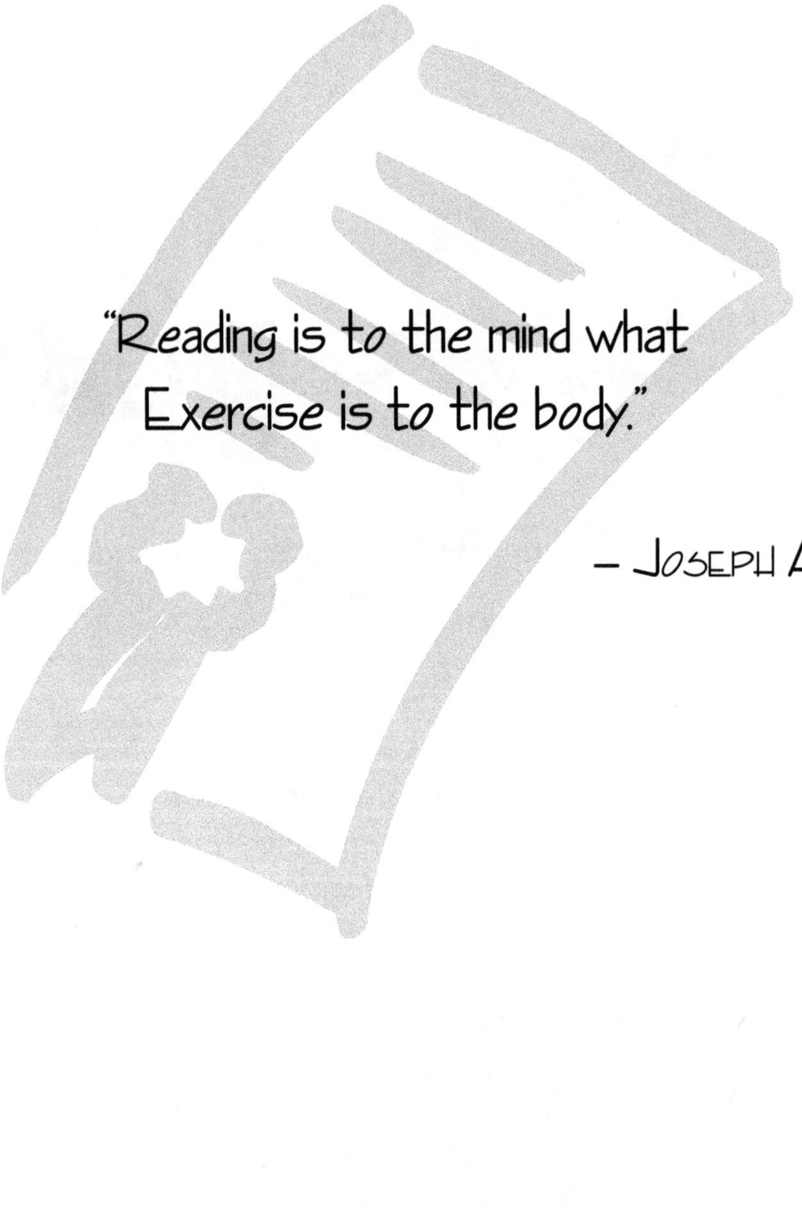

"Reading is to the mind what
Exercise is to the body."

– Joseph Addison

Action Steps

☐ Sunday ____________________

____

____

☐ Monday ____________________

____

____

☐ Tuesday ____________________

____

____

☐ Wednesday ____________________

____

____

☐ Thursday ____________________

____

____

☐ Friday ____________________

____

____

☐ Saturday ____________________

____

____

July

Read

Week 2

Positive Reinforcement

☐ Sunday ______________________________

☐ Monday ______________________________

☐ Tuesday ______________________________

☐ Wednesday ______________________________

☐ Thursday ______________________________

☐ Friday ______________________________

☐ Saturday ______________________________

July

Read

week 3

Role Playing

☐ Sunday ______________________

____

____

☐ Monday ______________________

____

____

☐ Tuesday ______________________

____

____

☐ Wednesday ______________________

____

____

☐ Thursday ______________________

____

____

☐ Friday ______________________

____

____

☐ Saturday ______________________

____

____

July

Read

week 4

Growing

- [ ] Sunday

- [ ] Monday

- [ ] Tuesday

- [ ] Wednesday

- [ ] Thursday

- [ ] Friday

- [ ] Saturday

July

Notes

July Notes cont.

AUGUST

The Positive Word Seed: sharing

TEACHERS:

Other words: collaborate, cooperate, participate, exchange, generosity, graciousness and appreciation.

share

Function: *verb*

Inflected Form(s): shared; shar·ing

Date: 1590

transitive verb

1 : to divide and distribute in shares : apportion —usually used with *out* <*shared* out the land among his heirs>

2 a : to partake of, use, experience, occupy, or enjoy with others b : to have in common <they share a passion for opera>

3 : to grant or give a share in —often used with with <*shared* the last of her water with us>

4 : to tell (as thoughts, feelings, or experiences) to others —often used with with*intransitive verb*

1 : to have a share —used with *in* <we all *shared* in the fruits of our labor>

2 : to apportion and take shares of something

3 : to talk about one's thoughts, feelings, or experiences with others

— shar·er *noun*

Teacher's Quote

"We are only fully alive when we're helping others."

– Rick Warren

Kids' Quote

Alone we can do so little.
Together we can do so much.

- Helen Keller

Action Steps

☐ Sunday ______________________________

____

____

☐ Monday ______________________________

____

____

☐ Tuesday ______________________________

____

____

☐ Wednesday ______________________________

____

____

☐ Thursday ______________________________

____

____

☐ Friday ______________________________

____

____

☐ Saturday ______________________________

____

____

August

sharing

week 2

Positive Reinforcement

☐ Sunday ______________________________

☐ Monday ______________________________

☐ Tuesday ______________________________

☐ Wednesday ______________________________

☐ Thursday ______________________________

☐ Friday ______________________________

☐ Saturday ______________________________

Role Playing

☐ Sunday

☐ Monday

☐ Tuesday

☐ Wednesday

☐ Thursday

☐ Friday

☐ Saturday

August

sharing

week 4

Growing

☐ Sunday

☐ Monday

☐ Tuesday

☐ Wednesday

☐ Thursday

☐ Friday

☐ Saturday

August

Notes

August Notes cont.

SEPTEMBER

The Positive Word Seed: Respect

TEACHERS:
Other words: Appreciate consideration, heed, honor, value.

re·spect
Pronunciation: \ri-'spekt\
Function: *noun*
Etymology: Middle English, from Latin *respectus*, literally, act of looking back, from *respicere* to look back, regard, from *re-* + *specere* to look — more at spy
Date: 14th century

1 : a relation or reference to a particular thing or situation <remarks having respect to an earlier plan>
2 : an act of giving particular attention : consideration
3 a : high or special regard : esteem
b : the quality or state of being esteemed
c *plural* : expressions of respect or deference <paid our respects>

Teacher's Quote

"To handle yourself, use your head;
To handle others, use you heart."

– Donald Anderson Laird

Kids' Quote

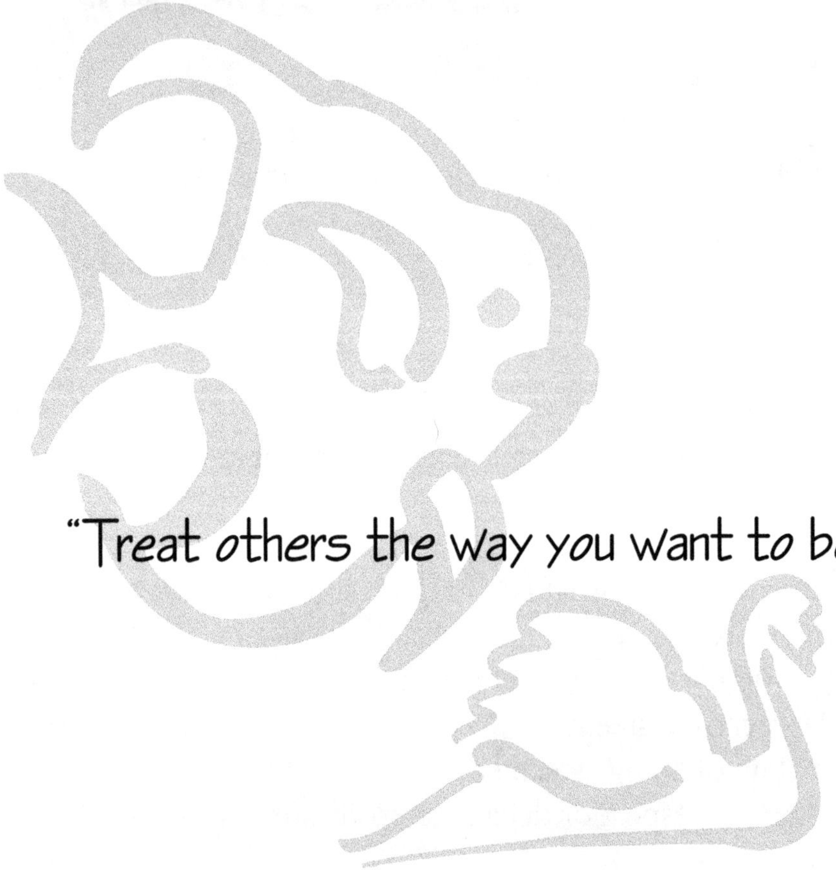

"Treat others the way you want to be treated."

- Holy Bible

Action Steps

☐ Sunday ______________________________

____

____

☐ Monday ______________________________

____

____

☐ Tuesday ______________________________

____

____

☐ Wednesday ______________________________

____

____

☐ Thursday ______________________________

____

____

☐ Friday ______________________________

____

____

☐ Saturday ______________________________

____

____

Positive Reinforcement

☐ Sunday ______________________________

____

____

☐ Monday ______________________________

____

____

☐ Tuesday ______________________________

____

____

☐ Wednesday ______________________________

____

____

☐ Thursday ______________________________

____

____

☐ Friday ______________________________

____

____

☐ Saturday ______________________________

____

____

Role Playing

☐ Sunday ______________________________

____

____

☐ Monday ______________________________

____

____

☐ Tuesday ______________________________

____

____

☐ Wednesday ______________________________

____

____

☐ Thursday ______________________________

____

____

☐ Friday ______________________________

____

____

☐ Saturday ______________________________

____

____

Growing

☐ Sunday

☐ Monday

☐ Tuesday

☐ Wednesday

☐ Thursday

☐ Friday

☐ Saturday

september

Notes

September Notes cont.

OCTOBER

The Positive Word Seed: Think

TEACHERS:

Other words: contemplate, comprehend, evaluate.

think

Pronunciation: \'thiŋk\

Function: *verb*

Inflected Form(s): thought \'thȯt\; think·ing

Etymology: Middle English *thenken*, from Old English *thencan*; akin to Old High German *denken* to think, Latin **tongēre** to know — more at thanks

Date: before 12th century

transitive verb

1 : to form or have in the mind

2 : to have as an intention <*thought* to return early>

3 a : to have as an opinion <think it's so> b : to regard as : consider <think the rule unfair>

4 a : to reflect on : ponder <think the matter over> b : to determine by reflecting <think what to do next>

5 : to call to mind : remember <he never thinks to ask how we do>

6 : to devise by thinking —usually used with up <*thought* up a plan to escape>

7 : to have as an expectation : anticipate <we didn't think we'd have any trouble>

8 a : to center one's thoughts on <talks and thinks business> b : to form a mental picture of

9 : to subject to the processes of logical thought <think things out>

Kids' Quote

"Change your thoughts,
And you can change your world."

– Norman Vincent Peale

Think

Action Steps

☐ Sunday ____________________

____

____

☐ Monday ____________________

____

____

☐ Tuesday ____________________

____

____

☐ Wednesday ____________________

____

____

☐ Thursday ____________________

____

____

☐ Friday ____________________

____

____

☐ Saturday ____________________

____

____

Positive Reinforcement

☐ Sunday ______________________________

____

____

☐ Monday ______________________________

____

____

☐ Tuesday ______________________________

____

____

☐ Wednesday ______________________________

____

____

☐ Thursday ______________________________

____

____

☐ Friday ______________________________

____

____

☐ Saturday ______________________________

____

____

October

Think

Week 3

Role Playing

☐ Sunday ______________________________

____

____

☐ Monday ______________________________

____

____

☐ Tuesday ______________________________

____

____

☐ Wednesday ______________________________

____

____

☐ Thursday ______________________________

____

____

☐ Friday ______________________________

____

____

☐ Saturday ______________________________

____

____

October

Think

week 4

Growing

☐ Sunday

☐ Monday

☐ Tuesday

☐ Wednesday

☐ Thursday

☐ Friday

☐ Saturday

october

Notes

October Notes cont.

NOVEMBER

The Positive Word Seed: Thankful

TEACHERS:
Other words: grateful, obliged, pleased and relieved.

thank·ful

Pronunciation: \'thaŋk-fəl\
Function: *adjective*
Date: before 12th century

1 : conscious of benefit received <for what we are about to receive make us truly thankful>
2 : expressive of thanks <thankful service>
3 : well pleased : glad <was thankful that it didn't rain>
— thank·ful·ness *noun*

Teacher's Quote

"Nothing is more honorable than a grateful heart."

– Seneca the Elder
(Roman Philosopher, ca 54 BC - ca 39 AD)

Kids' Quote

"In all things give thanks."

- Holy Bible

November Thankful week 1

Action Steps

☐ Sunday ______________________________

____

____

☐ Monday ______________________________

____

____

☐ Tuesday ______________________________

____

____

☐ Wednesday ______________________________

____

____

☐ Thursday ______________________________

____

____

☐ Friday ______________________________

____

____

☐ Saturday ______________________________

____

____

November Thankful Week 2

Positive Reinforcement

☐ Sunday ____

____

____

☐ Monday ____

____

____

☐ Tuesday ____

____

____

☐ Wednesday ____

____

____

☐ Thursday ____

____

____

☐ Friday ____

____

____

☐ Saturday ____

____

____

Role Playing

☐ Sunday ____________________

☐ Monday ____________________

☐ Tuesday ____________________

☐ Wednesday ____________________

☐ Thursday ____________________

☐ Friday ____________________

☐ Saturday ____________________

November Thankful week 4

Growing

☐ Sunday ______

☐ Monday ______

☐ Tuesday ______

☐ Wednesday ______

☐ Thursday ______

☐ Friday ______

☐ Saturday ______

DECEMBER

The Positive Word Seed: growth

growth
Pronunciation: \'grōth\
Function: *noun*
Date: 1557

1 a (1) : a stage in the process of growing : size (2) : full growth
b : the process of growing
c : progressive development : evolution
d : increase, expansion <the growth of the oil industry>
2 a : something that grows or has grown
b : an abnormal proliferation of tissue (as a tumor)
c : outgrowth d : the result of growth : product
3 : a producing especially by growing <fruits of his own growth>
4 : anticipated progressive growth especially in capital value and income <some investors prefer growth to immediate income>

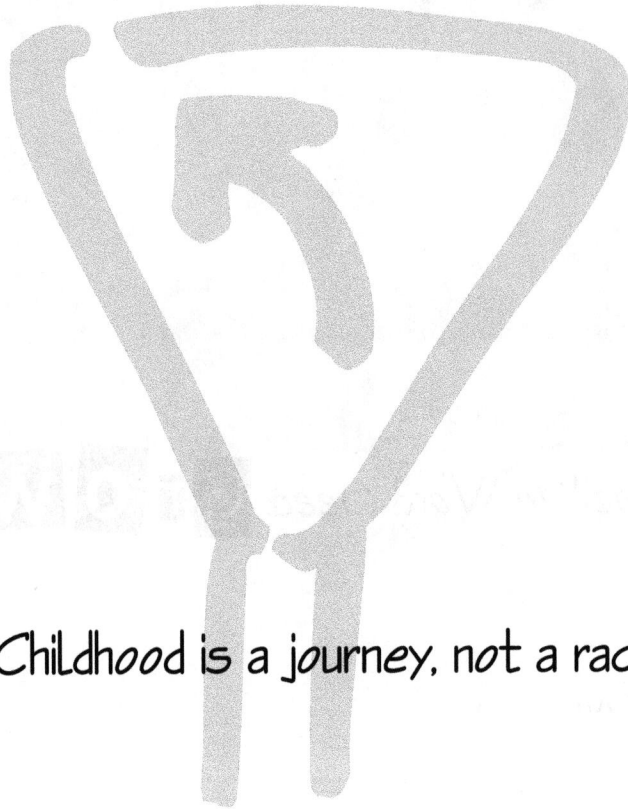

Kids' Quote

"Childhood is a journey, not a race.

- Unknown

Action Steps

☐ Sunday

☐ Monday

☐ Tuesday

☐ Wednesday

☐ Thursday

☐ Friday

☐ Saturday

Positive Reinforcement

☐ Sunday ______________________________

☐ Monday ______________________________

☐ Tuesday ______________________________

☐ Wednesday ______________________________

☐ Thursday ______________________________

☐ Friday ______________________________

☐ Saturday ______________________________

Role Playing

☐ Sunday ______________________________

____

____

☐ Monday ______________________________

____

____

☐ Tuesday ______________________________

____

____

☐ Wednesday ______________________________

____

____

☐ Thursday ______________________________

____

____

☐ Friday ______________________________

____

____

☐ Saturday ______________________________

____

____

Growing

☐ Sunday

☐ Monday

☐ Tuesday

☐ Wednesday

☐ Thursday

☐ Friday

☐ Saturday

December

Notes

December Notes cont.

To order additional copies of

Ms. Sally's

Healthy Habit

CALENDAR JOURNAL For Kids

TEACHER'S GUIDE

have your credit card ready and call
From USA: 1 800-917-BOOK (2665)
From Canada: (877) 855-6732

or e-mail
orders@selahbooks.com

or order online at
www.selahbooks.com

www.ingramcontent.com/pod-product-compliance
Lightning Source LLC
Chambersburg PA
CBHW062049090426
42740CB00016B/3069